AF428250

Fancy's Parade Party

Written and Illustrated by Robyn Fiebelkorn

For more information or to contact the author,
Robyn Fiebelkorn email: rfiebelkorn23@gmail.com

Cover art and illustrations: Robyn Fiebelkorn
Design: Russel Davis, Bravo Book Design

Softcover ISBN: 979-8-9911620-0-5
Hardcover ISBN: 979-8-9911620-1-2

Printed in the United States of America

Published by
Robyn Fiebelkorn
Spokane, Washington

Author's Page

It's always been a dream of mine to write and illustrate
Children's picture books. I love being a Nana. Cooking
for friends and family makes me happy. The connection
between food and conversation is priceless. I have
drawn pictures and used watercolor for most of my
life. My husband and I live in the Pacific Northwest.
We are blessed with two daughters and five wonderful
grandchildren.

I'm Nana with a blind disabled grandchild. It's
important to me that all children feel loved and accepted.
Children are the future. Let's take care of them.

Dedication

To all the children in this world.
YOU ARE LOVED. YOU ARE IMPORTANT.
YOU ARE WHO YOU WERE MEANT TO BE.

Acknowledgments

This is my granddaughter Leonna's story. Leonna has
enjoyed helping bring Fancy to life as a Fancy Chicken
who's confidence and talents makes friends and family
very happy. Thank you, Leonna.

This book would not have been possible without
the best support system ever. My family and friends
have cheered me on with great enthusiasm. From
brainstorming, editing, perfecting the recipe and reading
it countless times, this book is better because of you. A
special shout out to my daughter Heidi, my brother Tim
and my brother Neil. Many, many thanks to each of you.
You are appreciated.

Fancy's Parade Party

To:

From:

Date:

On a sunny farm,
there lived a chicken named Fancy.

She loves all her barnyard friends
and Hank the Fox.

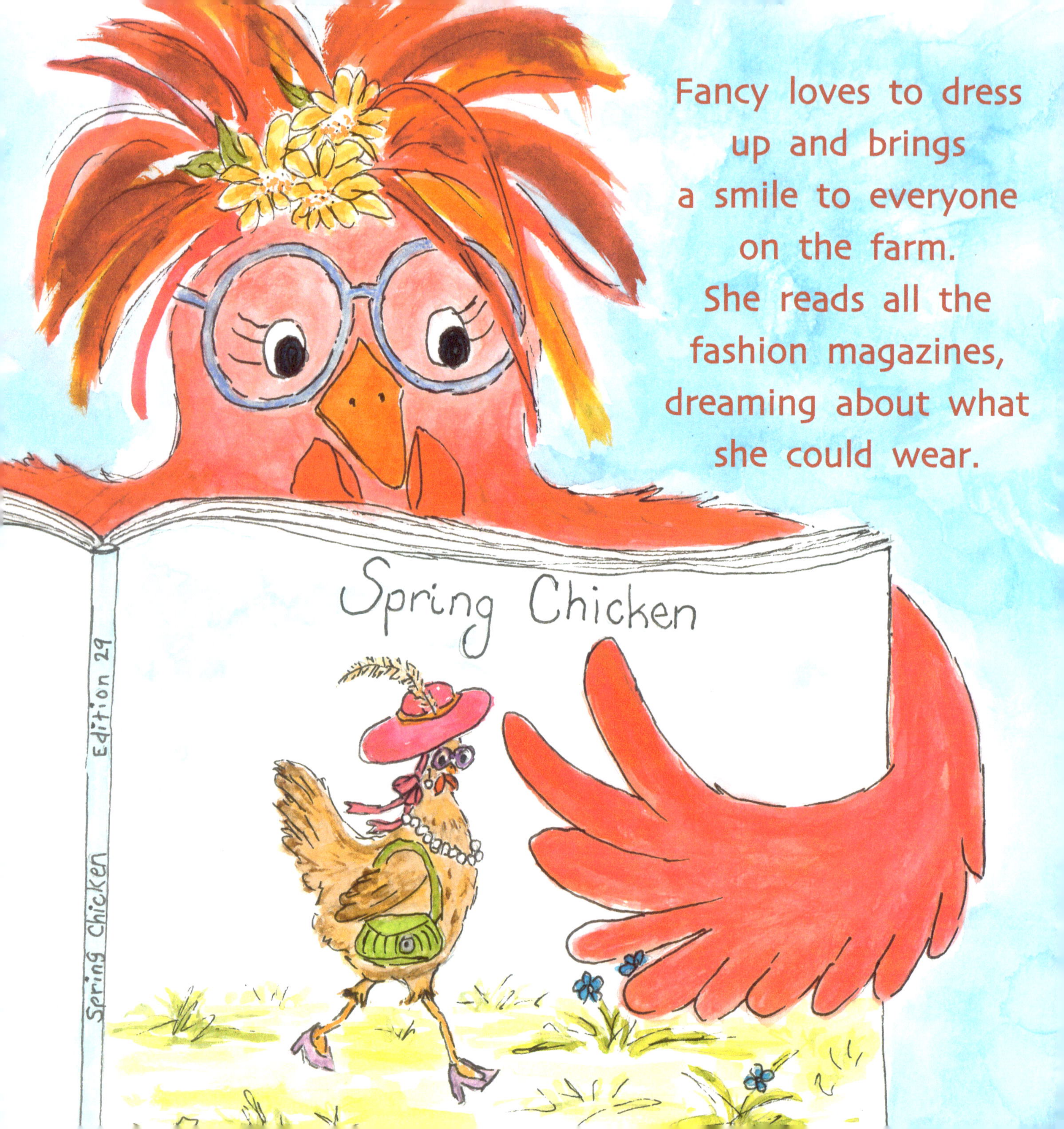

Fancy loves to dress
up and brings
a smile to everyone
on the farm.
She reads all the
fashion magazines,
dreaming about what
she could wear.

Feather Fashions
Feather Fashions
Pretty Poutry
Glam Glasses
Fancy Tutu's
Chic Chicken
The dressed Hen
Rowdy Rooster

What if all Fancy's friends
want to dress up too?

Fancy has an idea!

Fancy flutters around the farm singing,

"Let's have a parade!"

"Have you heard?

We're having a parade!"

"What is your favorite way to dress up?"

"Oh dear,
What shall I wear?"

Jack the rooster wants a crown.
Patty the cow wants flowers and ribbons.

maison d'œufs

With all her friends gathered,
Fancy clucks,
"Let the parade begin."

LOOK AT ME, I'M IN A PARADE!

THIS IS SO FUN,
IT'S A PARTY!
What is your favorite costume?

Herman the horse carries the littlest chick on the farm.

Hank the fox wears a dashing top hat,
Benny the pig, his purple glasses.
Can you find the fairy to make a wish?

A party always has cupcakes!

The chicks say,

"CUPCAKES! YES, PLEASE!"

Fancy beams with pride knowing that her idea
had brought so much joy to everyone.

What a great day!

maison d'oeufs
Fancy's favorite part
of each day comes
at the end,
when she sings a
lullaby to all the
baby chicks.

Fancy gathers all the baby chicks around her. The baby chicks snuggle closer, their tiny eyes getting sleepy as they listen to Fancy's sweet song. Her voice is gentle and soothing.

Hank and all her other
friends listen too.

Cluck Cluck Cluck
the stars and moon,
are shining bright

Cluck Cluck Cluck
close your eyes
and sleep so tight

Cluck Cluck Cluck
my sweet little darlings
I love you

Fancy's Party Cupcakes

Preheat oven to 350°

Batter
3/4 cup Butter Softened
1/4 cup oil
1 2/4 cups Sugar
Whip together until fluffy and light

Then add mixing in:
4 Eggs (one at a time)
1 cup Milk
2 teaspoon Vanilla

Mix thoroughly then add:
2 1/2 tsp Baking powder
1 teaspoon Salt
3 cups All-Purpose flour
Mix until smooth and add by hand
1/2 cup Rainbow sprinkles

Vanilla Buttercream Frosting
1 cup Butter room temp
2 Tablespoons Vanilla
2 1/2 cups powdered Sugar add 1 cup at a time
Whip until fluffy

Fill cupcake liners with batter 1/2 full
Bake for 15 – 20 minutes until the toothpick comes out clean.
Cool then frost with Buttercream
Top with sprinkles.

Fancy likes to set Frosted Cupcakes in the fridge for
30 – 60 minutes until chilled for a firmer buttercream.

Just like the real pastry chefs do it. **Enjoy!**

9 798991 162012